What Do You Do?

Written by Suzanne Hardin / Illustrated by Melissa Bay Mathis

CELEBRATION PRESS
Pearson Learning Group

Two for a crew,
two for a crew.

What do you do with
two for a crew?

Sail!

Four at the shore,
four at the shore.
What do you do with
four at the shore?

Swim!

Six on the bricks,
six on the bricks.
What do you do with
six on the bricks?

Fly!

Eight in a crate,
eight in a crate.
What do you do with
eight in a crate?

Run!

Ten in a den,
ten in a den.
What do you do with
ten in a den?

Sleep!

Twelve by themselves,
twelve by themselves.
What do you do with
twelve by themselves?

Waddle!

All you really have to do,
is practice how to count by twos.
2, 4, 6, 8, 10, and

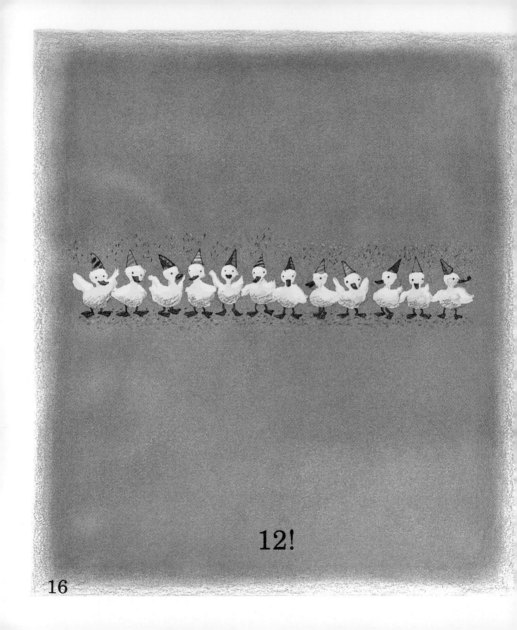

12!